Making Money with Chickens

How to make up to 12k per year with just 15 chickens

By Lisa Murano

Murano Chicken Farm

http://www.MuranoChickenFarm.com

For permissions contact: muranohatchery@gmail.com

Preface

I wrote this book for the homesteader or chicken keeper that already has chickens and wants them to start earning their keep. My methods were not devised to create a full-time job or income. I'm not saying you can't do that, but my methods were created to offset the cost of running a homestead. In this book I'll teach you how to make about $1000 a month with just 15 chickens. The money I make selling chicks completely pays the feed bills and some other bills on the homestead.

Chickens can be expensive. Even if you don't count the coop, the feed and bedding are monthly expenses that really add up! I decided a long time ago to have a no freeloader's policy and I make all my chickens earn their keep. I've tried many different ways to make money from my chickens, but the most profitable way just fell into my lap! In this book I'm going to explain exactly how I make money with my chickens. In fact, I'm going to break it down to exactly how you can make up to $12,000 a year with only 15 chickens.

I have operated a small-scale farm, turning a profit for over 5 years. In this book I will explain how to sell chicks, eggs, feathers and more to bring in money all year round. I will explain how to market your product in person and online. I will also describe not only how I stumbled into a chick selling business, but how you can replicate my success on your own small farm or homestead.

I hope all the answers that you're seeking on how to make money with backyard chickens are answered in these pages.

As you read through this book you may run into some terms you're not familiar with. I've included a glossary of incubation terms at the end of the book for your convenience.

My story

I first started raising chickens in 2009. I decided to hatch my first chicks from eggs. I ordered from a few well-known breeders. I wanted Silkies, my husband wanted French Black Copper Marans and we couldn't find either one locally. When word got out that I had hatched chicks, I started getting calls from people who wanted to buy them. Obviously, I wanted to keep those babies since I hatched them for my own use, but as soon as they were full grown I considered hatching some of their fertilized eggs. So, I test hatched their eggs and planned out my breeding groups. I started selling chicks about a year after those first chicks hatched. I sold every chick I could hatch from my 8 chickens using a 40 egg Styrofoam incubator.

That winter I found a trio of adult guineas on craigslist to help with our tick problem (guineas just love eating ticks).The guineas were really helping with the tick problem, so I decided to hatch more so they could cover all of our property. Things got a little out of hand at this point. I learned that almost everyone in my area had the French Guineas which don't breed well, which means the eggs hardly ever hatch. Nobody liked the fact that they couldn't hatch their own guinea keets and had to buy more each year. Since I happened to have purchased a trio of standard guineas, I had no problems hatching their eggs. There's a little luck in that part of my story obviously. By the end of that summer I had to put my foot down and refuse to sell any more keets! Demand had been so high that I hadn't been able to keep any for myself yet. The next year I had about 11 guineas in my flock. Once I started hatching all their eggs, business completely exploded and kept at a steady pace for about 5 years until I decided it was time to slow down hatching and write about it instead!

Looking back, 3 main things stand out as the main contributors to my success.

* Choosing 2 breeds of chickens that not only were rare in my area but also in demand.
* Not understanding guineas and getting the ones that could naturally breed in a place where they were in demand was pretty darn lucky.
* I'm kind of a big mouth on social media and people finding out about my poultry also contributed to the start of chick sales for me.

The rest was all trial and error along with several big and small mistakes that I've learned from. I've had to come up with alternative methods of selling chicks, back up plans and hold policies. I learned how to use hatching software, Google calendar and bookkeeping programs. I have also experimented with several breeds of chickens and different types of waterfowl to try to learn what sells well in my area.

Over the last 8 years I have raised over 2 dozen different breeds of chickens, ducks, geese, quail and button quail. Most of these were as pets, but we did breed Khaki Campbell ducks for awhile and they were quite popular. Currently I am focusing on getting my Silkies up to show quality again. I had them on hold the last 2 years, while I focused on breeding the d'Uccles. I added in some new blood this spring though and now they're bouncing back. I've made great progress with them and think I can hit this goal fairly soon. The Silkies and guineas are the only 2 flocks I plan to breed for the next year or so. However, I am constantly looking for new breeds that really catch my attention.

My next adventure may be to raise quail in a giant flight pen the size of a small barn. Or maybe I'll raise emus next, I haven't really decided.

I started a blog in 2010 to show people which chicks I had available as well as for a place to answer some of the more common questions that I was getting asked. I thought it would be easier to point them to a blog than to spend so much time answering the same questions again and again. It worked. I probably spend more time writing about chickens now than anything! In June of this year I wrote the blog post that prompted this book. Within a week, the blog post on making $1000 a month with chickens had gone semi-viral. I realized that this was a topic people wanted to learn more about and I set out to provide that information.

How much money can you make?

My calculations are going to focus on 15 chickens because I realized that even when I had 90 I was making most of my money from two of my breeding groups. To get a good fertility rate I have two roosters over 13 hens. Keep in mind though that 15 is an arbitrary number. You can choose to raise as many or as few as you'd like. It's not always the case that more chickens equals more money though. How much money you can make will always depend on a few factors...

·   How many hens are laying: Hens lay most frequently in their first 2 years of life, so a younger flock will give you more eggs to hatch.

·   Fertility rate: To keep the fertility rate high, you want no more than 8-10 hens per rooster. If you find that the fertility rate is low, you should add an extra rooster to the flock.

·   Incubation capacity: You can only hatch as many eggs as you can incubate, and we'll discuss this in Chapter 3.

·   Customers: The number of customers you can find to buy your chicks will also determine your final profit.

These 4 points must work together for you to make money with chickens. Many people get into chicken breeding slowly (as I did) and work out the kinks as they go. I highly recommend taking your time and working your way up to your full potential. However, if you do want to jump right in, let's discuss how much money you can make with 15 chickens.

With 13 hens, if every hen laid an average of 6 eggs a week we would have a total of 78 eggs. Since there are two roosters to 13 hens they should have a high rate of fertility. Take those 78 eggs and multiply it by the four weeks in a month, and now we have 312 eggs. In a perfect situation those 312 eggs would hatch, and the chicks would sell for $5 each. They would bring in $390 a week or $1,560 that month.

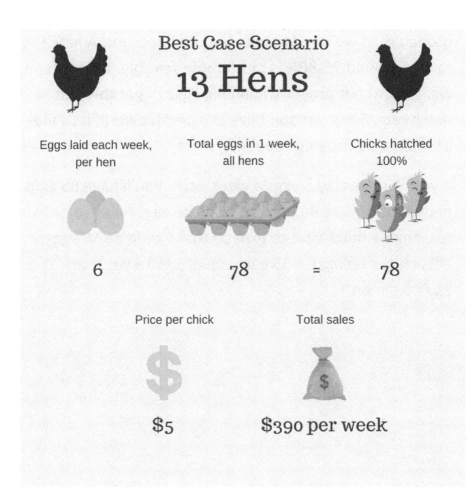

Best Case Scenario
13 Hens

| Eggs laid each week, per hen | Total eggs in 1 week, all hens | | Chicks hatched 100% |
| 6 | 78 | = | 78 |

| Price per chick | Total sales |
| $5 | $390 per week |

I know that sounds great, but it's probably not going to happen like that every month. I'm not trying to sell you on a perfect world scenario, I want you to understand what will probably happen and why. Chances are your hens are going to lay between 5-6 eggs a week each. As long as they are under 2 years old, they should lay at least 5 eggs a week. A 100% hatch rate every time is possible but not probable, so we need to take that into account. A hatch rate of around 75-80% is much more feasible. In chapter 8 we'll talk about properly handling eggs to get the best hatch rate. Since we don't live in a perfect world let's look at what will probably happen.

If your 13 hens lay 5 eggs a week each, you'll have 65 eggs per week. If 75 to 80 percent of those eggs hatch (a reasonable hatch rate to expect) that would be 50 eggs. Fifty chicks selling for $5 each equal $250 a week or $1,000 a month.

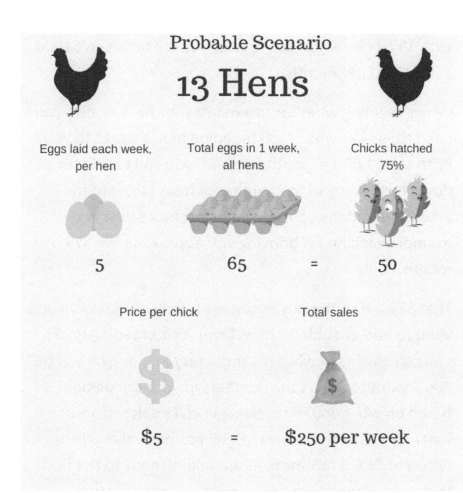

Probable Scenario

13 Hens

Eggs laid each week, per hen	Total eggs in 1 week, all hens		Chicks hatched 75%
5	65	=	50

Price per chick		Total sales
$5	=	$250 per week

Barring any drastic issues like incubator failure or predator attack, you're probably going to be somewhere in the middle of these 2 examples. If your hens regularly lay 6 eggs a week (which is very common in hens under 3 years old) and you get closer to a 90% hatch rate (very feasible with proper incubator settings and cleanliness) this equation brings us to $1,400 a month. As you can see, with 15 chickens you can regularly make between $1000 and $1,560 per month.

When deciding whether to expand your flock or not, you need to look at what each breeding hen is worth to you. With the $1,000 a month scenario, you can break this down by dividing in the number of hens (13) into the amount of money you receive from chick sales. In this example each hen is bringing you approximately $77 a month.

That $77 a month is an important number to know. If you want to add or subtract hens from your breeding flocks, you can easily see what the monetary loss or gain will be. You'll want to adjust the numbers in your calculations based on what you're receiving in chick sales. If your hatch rate is better or worse, the per hen value will be different. We'll talk more about adding hens to the flock in chapter 5 when we talk about flock maintenance.

Incubator capacity

Incubator capacity is important to determine both your potential income and your hatching schedule. Obviously, you're going to need an incubator or several. I have two Brinsea cabinet incubators that I absolutely love. I can rely on them completely and they are the 'set it and forget it' type. These types of incubators are programmed to be 99.5°F with forced air. All I do is add water for the humidity and a little display screen tells me how humid it is in the incubator. On day 19, I move the eggs into the hatching tray for lockdown and add water to raise the humidity. It's a very simple to use incubator, however, I started hatching with a 40 egg Styrofoam incubator. I had to baby that incubator a little bit, but I managed to get a good hatch rate from it.

Whether you decide to go with one big incubator or a couple of smaller incubators, keep in mind that each one has a maximum capacity. Incubation capacity is going to determine the maximum amount of money you can make. My maximum capacity with all my incubators is 600 eggs. I will never be able to have more than 600 eggs incubating at one time.

If I can only fit 600 eggs a month and expect about a 75% hatch rate, then only 450 eggs will become chicks. If I sell each chick for $5 then the most I can ever expect to make a month is $2,250.

If we're using one incubator that fits 40 eggs at a time: A 75% hatch rate means 30 of those eggs will hatch into chicks. Sell each of the chicks for $5 and make $150 per month.

You also must consider incubating space and hatching space. Is the incubator big enough to have eggs hatching at the same time other eggs are still incubating? Will you need a separate incubator to use as a hatcher? While many incubators have space for eggs to both incubate and hatch at the same time, varying humidity levels and the need to keep the incubator closed during lockdown could be a problem for developing eggs. It might be best to have two separate units.

Once I needed to hatch more eggs than a 40 egg incubator could hold, I bought a second one. I used one to incubate the eggs and the other to hatch them. I hatched eggs every week because demand was higher than my supply of eggs. When I had the two Styrofoam incubators I would set about 15 eggs a week. At the beginning of the week I had 3 sets of eggs in the first incubator and a fourth set of eggs in the second incubator that were hatching. After hatching was finished, I cleaned the incubator out and moved the next set of eggs into it. I then set a new batch of eggs in the first incubator.

You'll need to set eggs before they are 10 days old. We'll discuss how eggs are perishable and start to deteriorate after about 10 days in the chapter on handling hatching eggs. In order to get the best hatch rate, I set eggs weekly.

When you're just starting to sell chicks and don't have a steady stream of customers yet, you'll want to hatch less often to keep the work to a minimum. One big hatch is less work then 3 smaller hatches. If you have low incubator capacity and can fill it with fresh eggs in one hatch, then it would work out better for you to run one full hatch at a time. It's less work and less time invested in the hatches.

Often when I don't have a lot of demand for chicks I use an alternate week hatching schedule. I set eggs every other Friday so that chicks hatch on opposite weeks. This works out great if you only have one incubator, since you're not opening the incubator to turn eggs or set new eggs during the critical lock down phase of hatching.

Biweekly Hatching Schedule

SUN	MON	TUE	WED	THU	FRI	SAT
					SET HATCH #6	01
02	03	04 LOCK DOWN HATCH #5	05	06	07	08
09	10	11	12	13	14 SET HATCH #7	15
16	17	18 LOCK DOWN HATCH #6	19	20	21	22
23	24	25	26	27	28 SET HATCH #8	29
30	31	LOCK DOWN HATCH #7				

JULY 2016

In this instance you will have 2 sets of eggs in the incubator at one time. When you set the eggs for hatch 6, hatch 5 is already 2 weeks into incubation. If your incubator capacity is 40, you can only have 40 eggs between those two hatches.

When demand is high for chicks I use an every week schedule. This works best with 2 incubators, using one as the hatcher. Since the lockdown phase of incubation calls for higher humidity, I don't recommend hatching every week in the same incubator you're using for incubating the eggs. Exposure to high humidity for too long during hatching can cause problems with the developing e

Weekly Hatching Schedule

SUN	MON	TUE	WED	THU	FRI	SAT
						21
					SET HATCH #6	
02	03	04 LOCK DOWN HATCH #4	05	06	07 SET HATCH #7	08
09	10	11 LOCK DOWN HATCH #5	12	13	14 SET HATCH #8	15
16	17	18 LOCK DOWN HATCH #6	19	20	21 SET HATCH #9	22
23	24	25 LOCK DOWN HATCH #7	26	27	28 SET HATCH #10	29
30	31	LOCK DOWN HATCH #8				

JULY 2016

In this case you will have 5 sets of eggs incubating at one time. If your incubator capacity is 40, then each hatch would only have 8 eggs in it. However, if your incubators capacity is closer to 200, each hatch could have up to 40 eggs in it. When buying or building a new incubator keep incubation capacity in mind to determine what size you actually need.

Start up cost

If you are going to buy and build everything you need to breed 2 flocks of chickens, you would probably spend around $5000. Obviously most of that would be the chicken coops. It would take several months till you could start breeding, plus you wouldn't have enough buyers to be able to sell that many chicks just yet so you'd end up stuck with many of the chicks. It would also take quite a while to pay off your initial investment. While you can eventually pay off your investment and start making money selling chicks, not everybody has $5000 to throw at a new business only to have to wait months to actually make any money back. But, if you start with what you already have and build up your business as you go, that expense is a lot easier to take!

To minimize expenses you can start small. Start with a few chicks of the breed you've chosen and grow them out till they're ready to breed. As I mentioned in the beginning of the book, this was written for the homesteader or chicken keeper that already has some chickens. If you have chickens, you already have a coop, equipment, and maybe even an incubator. Work with what you have until your business grows enough that you need another incubator, or more hens in your breeding flock, or another coop. Expanding as the need arises keeps you from tying up a bunch of your own money at once.

To start with 15 good quality chicks from breeders, you'll probably spend less than $200 (Prices vary with breed and location).

When you're ready to test hatch, start with whatever incubator you have. You can build or buy one cheaply if you don't already have one. I've seen some amazing homemade incubator plans online! You can also utilize a broody for this if you have one. Once your business really starts going then you can invest in big cabinet incubators or larger coops. Remember to save receipts though, many expenses are deductible from your taxes.

Choosing breeds

The most important thing to determine when deciding what to sell is demand. You can have the most amazing flock of show quality chickens but if there is no demand for them you won't make any money. You will have to do a lot of research to determine which breeds would be a good fit for your area.

In the earlier calculations I mentioned selling your chicks for $5 each. I'm sure you've seen the bins of chicks available in your local feed store and you've noticed that they only charge about $3 each for them. In order to make money selling chicks, you're going to have to charge a little bit more for your chicks. The key to charging $5 or more per chick is to have the right breeds for your area. It also helps to have good quality specimens of those breeds. Show quality or breeder quality preferably. Nobody is going to pay you $2 more for a chick they can get at a feed store for $3, but if you have something that's a step above that or just hard to find, they will willingly pay more. I've seen breeder quality chicks go for $15 each! The opportunity to make money is there if you have good quality stock.

For example, my Silkies all came from breeders with very good reputations. I may have paid a little more per bird initially (and by a little more.... I mean a few dollars), but it pays off in the long run. My Silkies are all beautiful, fluffy and are a very good representation of the breed. These birds are exactly what people are looking for when they decide they want Silkies. This is why people will pay extra; your birds are exactly what they want! You simply figure out what they want in your area and you produce it, and customers will pay what you ask.

Another one of my flocks are the French black copper Marans. Marans are an interesting breed because they're mainly desired for their chocolate brown egg color. When breeding them I do like to avoid certain problems that they get with their feather coloring because I try to stay true to the breed. Mostly though I'm breeding for dark eggs which is simple enough.

The easiest of all my flocks are guinea fowl. There's no show quality and there's no pet quality, they're pretty much all the same which makes it really, really easy. I have seven colors and they all run together. What makes my guinea keets more in demand is that I have 7 colors while everybody else only has the standard pearl color. All I do is collect the eggs and hatch them. Guinea fowl are a perfect bird to make money on in my area because they're known to eat ticks and we have a bad tick problem around here.

It's important to mention that when I started breeding and selling from these flocks, I was the only one in the area. One of the reasons I managed to sell so many guinea keets for so long is because I have so many colors. However, when I started I only had the standard grey pearl, but as people saw me selling out at swaps they started raising and breeding them also. Once I had competition, I added pied, white and lavender colored guineas to my flock. Two years later I added royal purple and slate.

It took about 6 years, but my area is well saturated with guinea breeders now so I'm switching to a new breed for next year. The supply and demand are currently too close to make it an efficient breed to sell. Even though I am scaling back on guineas, I still expect to sell some since rural farmers need them to take care of the bugs. It helps if you live in a heavily tick populated area like I do here in Western Pennsylvania. As a chemical free pest solution, they practically sell themselves. I simply saw the demand and started supplying it.

Obviously, I prefer being the only one selling a particular breed. Unfortunately, with every breed I have tried in the area others have started selling the same breeds within a few years. At that point it's time to do some more research and move on to another breed or poultry type.

Now those are just the reasons why these flocks work for me. You may have people in your area that are absolutely nuts for Polish chickens. If that's what's going to sell, then I suggest that's what you get into if you're trying to make money selling chicks. You'll have to do some research. Join some local poultry groups online and in person and pay attention to 'wanted' and 'for sale' signs at feed stores. Attend auctions and poultry swap and take notes on what everybody is selling. Also take note of what is not selling, and which breeds aren't there at all. Think you might want to sell cochins? Start asking around if anybody knows where you can get cochins. Check craigslist and other online bulletin boards and sales groups. You need to get a feel for your area and what people are looking for.

You can still make money on the more common breeds, you just can't charge as much as you can with rare breeds. If you charge the same price or less than feed stores, you'll still sell a lot of birds! You may also be able to sell common breeds for a higher price if you live in an area that doesn't offer chick sales in feed stores.

I don't recommend what I call 'fad' chickens. It seems that every year there are new chickens that cost $100 each! People buy them up like crazy because they're rare and everybody wants to have them. It seems like these would be the most profitable chickens to breed, but they're not. They're over-bred like crazy and the quality suffers, plus the market tanks quickly. Next year it's going to be a different fad chicken. If you don't make your money back by then, you're not going to.

Another thing I recommend is to sell straight run chicks.

You want to avoid sex-links and other breeds that can be sexed at sight on hatch. Yes, you will lose a few sales because you can't provide all pullets. However, you'll lose even more money if you have to raise all the cockerels because nobody bought them. Also, be careful with letting people pick through your chicks. If somebody tries to sex a chick and doesn't know what they're doing, they could hurt it.

Most of my breeds cannot be sexed at hatch by the average person. I didn't do that intentionally, but I am glad it worked out that way. If by some chance I have chicks that don't sell and they grow out for a few months, I then sell the pullets for $10 and either give the cockerels away or take them to auction. Sometimes I grow them out for meat, depending on how many I have.

Setting up breeding groups

Housing

With the flock of 15 chickens example, you're going to be selling about 50 chicks a week. Trying to sell 50 chicks of 1 breed is harder than trying to sell 25 chicks each from 2 different breeds. A large quantity of 1 breed over-saturates your market quickly. If you don't have the market to sustain that amount of sales (and many do not) you'll need to set up two separate breeding flocks. Each flock will have 1 rooster. You could even break this down further into 3 breeding groups if your market isn't strong enough to support the sales of chicks from 2. In that case you'll need to add another rooster though, so you'll have 16 chickens for the earlier calculations to be exact.

For the sake of simplicity, let's just assume you're setting up 2 breeding groups. Let's say these 2 breeding groups are Group A with six hens and 1 rooster and Group B with seven hens and one rooster. That equals up to our 15 chickens. To keep each group a pure breed, you'll need to keep them separated. If the rooster from 1 flock mixes in with the other flock the chicks will not be purebred. It takes between 2-3 weeks for the hen to no longer be fertile by that rooster after mating occurs.

If one of your roosters gets in with the other flock, you cannot sell the chicks as purebred. I will still sell them but at a lower price. I usually get $2-$3 each for mutt chicks. Make sure you mention that it is a mix breed chick, so the buyer knows what to expect. If you know your chicks will not be purebred, you can also choose to not incubate the eggs for a few weeks.

To keep breeds from mixing, I have separate coops for each of my breeds. Each chicken coop has its own run. Each day 1 group stays in their coop and run and the other group can free range. I rotate which group gets to free range daily. Depending on the size of your property you may be able to have separate fenced in areas for them to free range in. I've also seen a setup with a coop split down the middle inside and each flock having their own run outside.

Some types of poultry can live together without breeding. If you decide to breed turkeys, ducks, geese, chickens, guineas, chukars, quail, peafowl etc. then you can often put 2 different types in one coop. I've always had guineas and chickens in the same coop. I've also had ducks in the coop with chickens and guineas for a short while. I prefer to keep most of mine separate, but it is possible to keep 2 flocks in the same coop if their different varieties of poultry. Take a look around at what you have available to work with and if you can house separate flocks without them mixing. It's not unusual to start with one breed in one coop and expand as time and income allows.

Breeding

To start my flocks, I chose 2 breeders to buy eggs from for each breed. I purchased 1 dozen hatching eggs from each breeder. I grew these chicks out and chose which chickens I wanted to breed based on how the breed was supposed to look.

When deciding which chickens to keep for breeding you'll want to look at the APA and the standards they use. The American Standard of Perfection (commonly referred to as just The Standard) classifies and describes the standard physical appearance, coloring and temperament for all recognized breeds of poultry. It is used by American Poultry Association judges at sanctioned poultry shows. There are nearly 60 breeds in the most recent edition which was published in 2010. Basically, this is the final word in what your breed of chicken should look like. You'll only want to breed chickens that are good specimens of your chosen breed and The Standard can help you to identify which ones they are. You'll obviously want to remove any chickens with deformities or flaws from your breeding groups, but having a breed standard can help you to identify some of the less obvious flaws in your particular breed.

I've found a lot of great information on my chosen breeds by looking up that breed's official group or organization. You'll find lots of information about the breed which can help guide your breeding choices. Many groups also have breeder's directories which can be a good resource when looking to add to your flock.

Occasionally you'll find that one of your hens looks perfect herself, but is giving you flawed chicks. She will need to be removed from your breeding group to maintain the quality of the chicks. One of my Silkie hens was giving me light skinned chicks, which is a definite flaw for Silkies. To determine which hen it is, I separate a few girls at night when they go to roost. I'll put them in a large cage with food and water. I let them out after they lay their eggs the next day. Do this with the same hens for 5 days. Mark their egg and set them in the incubator. Switch those hens out for another group for the next 5 days. Since it takes 21 days to hatch it will take a few weeks, but you'll eventually figure out which group the flawed chicks are coming from.

Take that group and separate them 1 by 1 till you figure out who it is. When you find the hen that is producing the flawed chicks, move her out of the breeding group. Either sell her as a layer (I always disclose about breeding flaws-- most people don't care) or keep her for laying eggs for consumption. By using this method, I can continue to hatch chicks while I figure out who needs to be removed from the breeding flock.

You can still sell your test hatches even if they're not

ideal! I have sold many chicks that were less than my idea of quality, I just sell them at a discount. I will knock down the price because leg feathering isn't correct, or skin coloring is off. I always let the buyer know WHY I'm selling them for a reduced price. People are happy to get a bargain, but you want them to know what to expect so they don't think that's your standard of quality. People will talk, and you don't want them bad mouthing you to others because it hurts your income! Honesty is always best, and I think you'll find most people aren't sticklers for breed type, as long as they've been informed.

Record keeping

I like to keep records on the origin and breed pairings of my chickens. This helps to insure the genetics inside the group is not closely related. If I keep any of my own chicks, I record their parent's if possible. Many times, I only have the hen group and the rooster info since I can't always tell which chick came from which hen. I use leg bands on my hens, so I can tell them apart. This number is also on their records. You can choose to record as much or as little info as you think is relevant, as long as the info you need to guide your breeding choices is written down. Don't make the mistake of thinking you will remember it all. Trying to recall all the breeders, flocks and pairings will become impossible and you'll end up having to guess which could turn out poorly. This information is also important if I decide to try a new breeding method.

Breeding methods

I currently use a method called pen mating with my chickens. I chose this method in the beginning for its simplicity. When pen mating, choose a rooster unrelated to your hens and put them all together in the same pen to mate. It's a very simple method to use and the main downside is that you will not know exactly which hen a particular chick is from for record keeping.

Another fairly simple method is flock mating. This is very similar to pen mating except there are multiple roosters. This works well with larger flocks, but the downside is you are never sure which mating an individual chick is from.

If you have a way to separate a few smaller groups of the same flock, consider clan mating (also called spiral mating). This requires a few more roosters and lots of record keeping but you can really improve your flock this way.

There are many different breeding methods you can use and trying to describe them all is way outside the scope of this book. I suggest you do some research on different breeding methods before deciding on which one to use.

Flock maintenance
Hens lay eggs most reliably in the first 2 years of their

lives. After 2 years their production dips and they will lay less eggs each year as time goes on. I like to add 4 to 6 new pullets every year. When I add new layers to the flock, I remove that many of the oldest hens. They are sold off as 2 year old layers. I have not had any trouble selling them at all. In fact, since they have a great reputation as coming from my breeding groups I can usually get a lot more for them then a regular hen or pullet. Of course, sometimes this ends up creating competition for myself, but I try to continuously improve my lines, so the competition doesn't bother me much.

If you do not add new layers to your flock, then as the flock ages they will lay fewer eggs every year and your income will go down. If you want to keep production up, you will need to add new layers regularly.

When I add new chickens to my flock I like to add new bloodlines. I have a few breeders I like to work with because I have had good experiences with them. I try not to go to the same breeder more than every other year.

The most important things to think about when adding to your breeding flock is breed improvement. You don't want to add in any chickens that are inferior to the ones in your flock already. The quality of chicks you produce will rarely stay the same. It will either improve or decrease with each new flock member. Since I want to be able to charge more for chicks, I always try to add flock members that will improve the quality of the chicks I'm hatching. Use your breed standard to determine which chickens most closely meet the specifications for the breed you're working with.

Collecting hatching eggs

You'll need to collect eggs daily, preferably twice a day. I collect in the morning and again at mid-afternoon, though evening might work better for you. In average weather conditions, that will suffice. However, in the cold of winter or the heat of summer, eggs that are left all day could become too cold to develop or too warm and may even start to develop in the nest box.

Winter:

Eggs that freeze and crack should be discarded. Remember, chickens walk through poop and dirt all day long. Even if you keep their nest boxes sparkling clean, they will have bacteria in them. You wouldn't want to incubate a split egg that has poo bacteria in it because it could spread bacteria throughout the incubator and effect the whole hatch. Frozen eggs that don't crack will not develop and hatch. To prevent freezing, eggs should be collected 3 times a day when temperatures are below freezing.

Summer:

Ideally eggs should be stored at a humid 55-65°F. In the hottest months of summer, the outdoor temperatures can be much warmer than this. Eggs kept too warm for too long can begin to lose interior quality. Also, if they stay warm for an extended period, your fertile eggs might begin to develop all on their own! When you then bring them inside to store until you're ready to incubate them, they will stop developing. The cells that have started to form will die off and the egg will not be able to develop into a chick. To prevent issues in the summer, eggs should be collected 3 times a day.

Fall & Spring:

Morning and night gathering should suffice as long as the nest boxes are kept clean.

Other reasons for collecting eggs frequently:

Egg eaters: To prevent chickens from becoming egg eaters, the eggs should be removed often.

Poop: The longer the eggs remain in the nest box, the more chance that someone may get feces on them.

Bacteria: Bacteria can be carried into the nest boxes by the chickens, especially on their feet. Since bacteria can't be seen by the naked eye it is not easily removed. The longer the eggs sit there the more hens visit the nest, the higher chance of bacteria getting on the egg.

Temperature fluctuations: Eggs should be stored at either room temperature or refrigerated. When sitting in the coop for several days they are exposed to air temperature fluctuations. If it gets up to 70 during the day but back down to 40 at night, that's too much of a temperature change. A cold egg that warms up can sweat which can facilitate the growth of bacteria.

Predators: Snakes love eggs. Leave eggs around too long and a snake might find them. Predators generally remember where they got their last free meal, so if a snake finds them once he'll be back! Other predators like opossums, raccoons, skunks and rats also like eggs.

Breakage: Hens move eggs around to make room for themselves and their new egg. Eggs break when knocked together. Broken eggs get eaten which encourages egg eating of unbroken eggs. Broken eggs can also get onto other eggs which can introduce bacteria into those eggs and then into your incubator.

Broodyness: Some people swear that leaving a clutch of eggs out will encourage a hen to go broody. I can't agree or disagree with this one as it is a hormonal change. However, broody hens do not lay eggs for a few months and since you're counting on those eggs I don't take the chance.

Handling hatching eggs

After collecting the eggs, I place them pointy side down in egg cartons in a room which stays around 60°F. They should be stored in about 75% humidity with a temperature between 55-65°F. Since eggs are porous, humidity keeps the egg from losing moisture. Temperatures below 65°F keep the egg from starting to develop too soon. Temperatures below 55°F destroy the eggs ability to develop.

Do not wash eggs before incubating. Washing the eggs washes away the 'bloom' and allows bacteria to enter the egg. Just brush off any dirt or scrape it off with a fingernail. Don't set the egg if you think it's too dirty. You don't want to introduce bacteria into your incubator which could ruin your whole hatch. Because of this reason, always wash my hands before and after handling hatching eggs.

I do not use odd shaped eggs, or eggs that are abnormally small or large. Larger eggs often have double yolks which very rarely hatch. Odd shaped eggs won't allow the chick proper room to grow and it may die in the egg or be malformed. Unless you have a lot of extra incubator space, eliminating the eggs that have a low chance of hatching will free up space for eggs that will hatch.

I like to rotate the eggs daily during storage. To make this easy I place a 2" X 4" board under one end of the carton.

Switch the board to the opposite end each day so the carton is at a slight angle.

Don't incubate eggs older than 10 days. The hatch rate decreases after that. The egg begins to breakdown as it gets older and there is less of a chance it will develop and hatch. I set eggs every week to avoid this.

Choosing your incubator

There are two types of incubators. Forced air and still air. Still air means there is no artificial air flow inside the incubator. Forced air means that the incubator has a fan inside it to circulate the air. It's important to know what kind of incubator you have because the temperature requirements are different for each one.

A forced air incubator should be kept at 99-99.5° F. A still air incubator should be kept at 101-102° F at the top of the eggs. In a still air incubator you want to measure the air at the top of the eggs. Since the heat is coming from above, the eggs are warmer at the top them at the bottom. In a forced air incubator you can measure the air temperature anywhere inside the incubator, and it will be accurate since the air is circulating. I've had the best hatch rates with forced air incubators. It's very important to keep the air inside the incubator stable as even a one degree difference can terminate the embryos.

All incubators should have vent holes. Allowing fresh air into the incubator is essential. This allows oxygen to come in and the carbon dioxide produced by the developing eggs to go out.

You'll need both a thermometer and a hygrometer. A thermometer will measure the temperature inside the incubator. A hygrometer measures the humidity level inside the incubator. Humidity is also important during hatch. During incubation the humidity is kept between 40-50% for the first 18 days of incubation. The humidity is raised to 65% for the last 3 days off hatching. This varying level of humidity is why a separate hatcher is a good idea. If your incubator does not have a thermometer or hygrometer built in, you'll need to buy them to place inside the incubator.

Some incubators have egg turners. Eggs are placed in the turners and it does all the work of turning the eggs for you. If your incubator does not have an egg turner, then you will have to lay the eggs on their side and turn them by hand. Eggs must be turned during the first 18 days of incubation to insure the chick develops properly. If the egg is not turned often enough, the developing embryo can stick to the shell membrane causing abnormal growth. I turn my eggs 3 or 5 times a day. Always turn them an odd number of turns each day. Obviously, the eggs will not be turned while you're sleeping. By turning them an odd number of turns during the day, it is insured they will rest on opposite sides each night. You do not want them resting on the same side 2 nights in a row. To insure the eggs are turned fully I use a pencil to write an X on one side and an O on the other. If you are not going to be able to turn the eggs several times a day, choose an incubator with a turner.

Many of today's incubators are fully automatic with built

in thermometers, hygrometers, turners and forced air. You only have to add the eggs and water. While these are more expensive than basic or homemade models, they are much easier to use. I use the Brinsea line of incubators exclusively and have had great experience with them.

Incubators come in various sizes from small ones that only fit 7 eggs to cabinet incubators that fit several hundred eggs. Obviously, the largest incubators are quite expensive, so you'll want to make sure you have a good business plan and customer base before spending the money for one.

How to incubate eggs

Choose clean eggs that are less than 10 days old to incubate. Do not wash the eggs. Washing eggs removes the bloom which is a natural, protective coating. Do not incubate cracked, damaged or misshapen eggs. The eggs should be room temperature before setting them in the incubator. Place the eggs pointed end down in the turner, or lay them on their sides if there is no turner.

Turn your incubator on 24-48 hours before setting eggs. Check the temperature several times and make sure it stays steady for at least 12 hours before setting eggs. The incubator should be kept at 99-99.5° F for forced air and 101-102° F for a still air incubator.

The temperature inside your incubator will drop when you first put the new eggs in it. This is normal. Do not touch the controls, it will come back to the correct temperature as soon as the eggs warm up.

A chicken egg incubates for around 21 days to form a chick. I say 'around' because they can hatch up to 2 days early or 2 days late and still be considered on time.

Keep the humidity in the incubator between 40-50% for the first 18 days. When an egg is laid an air bubble forms inside it, this is called the air cell. This air cell is located at the large end of the egg. It is positioned between the shell and the membrane that contains the egg white and yolk.

This air cell helps to alleviate stress and pressure on the embryo as it grows. The chick will break through this membrane to hatch. The air cell get larger as the incubation time passes. Not enough humidity in the incubator and the air cell grows too big. Too much humidity and the air cell does not grow at all.

If the air cell doesn't grow big enough, the chick might not be able to reach it to break through it and can pip internally and drown in excess fluid. If the air cell is too big, it might trap the chick under it with no room to move to hatch. With correct humidity, the bubble will grow properly and this won't be an issue.

If your incubator does not have an egg turner, turn the eggs 3-5 times a day as discussed in the previous chapter.

I like to candle my eggs after 1 week of incubation. Using a strong flashlight or a candling light, look inside the egg. It helps if you're in a dark room. You should see a darkened blob with what looks like a red spider. It might also have a black spot in it. Dispose of any eggs that are not developing. Return the developing eggs to the incubator. Try to move quickly so the eggs do not get too cold.

On day 18 stop turning the eggs. If you have a removable turner, take it out. If your eggs are in turning trays (like in a cabinet incubator) move them to the hatching tray to hatch. Raise the humidity in the incubator to 65%. I like to put a piece of non-slip material in the bottom of the hatcher (under the eggs) so the chicks can get a good grip with their little feet. Rubber shelf liner works great for this.

From day 18 until about day 24 is considered "lock down". This is the crucial time while the chicks are hatching. If you open the incubator during this time, it will let the humidity out drying the membrane of the hatching chicks. Once the membrane dries, the chicks are unable to move and can get stuck in their shells. This is called shrink wrapped.

To raise humidity in the incubator, add water to the water reservoir. If you can't get the humidity to 65% with the water reservoir alone, you can also add a piece of wet sponge. To lower humidity, open the air vents.

Somewhere around day 21, the chick will peck a hole in the egg with the little egg tooth on his beak. This is called pipping. Sometimes you will hear cheeping even before they pip through the shell! After the chick pips through the shell, it will slowly peck its way around the shell breaking through the shell all the way around. This is called zipping. The chick will then push the top off the egg and pop out.

There really is no 'typical' hatch. Sometimes a chick will

pip and zip in an hour. Others will pip then rest a few hours before they start zipping. Others will partially zip then rest. It's not uncommon for a chick to take up to 24 hours to hatch.

Leave hatched chicks in the incubator until they're completely dry and fluffy. It can take up to 24 hours for them to fluff up.

If you have never incubated before, I do not recommend that you start incubating with pricey breeder eggs. I wasted a lot of money on quality eggs that way. I recommend you incubate a few hatches of cheaper eggs first until you get your hatching method figured out. If you have your own mixed flock that would be the obvious choice. You could also pick up a dozen eggs cheaply at a swap or auction while you're out doing your breed research.

The NPIP program

NPIP stands for National Poultry Improvement Plan, and it's a voluntary certification system that poultry breeders and hatcheries can choose to participate in. Requirements to join the NPIP vary by state and county. Your county department of agriculture will probably be handling your application. To be NPIP certified you would submit your flock to be tested for Fowl Typhoid and Salmonella Pullorum. You could also opt to have your flock tested for additional diseases like Avian Influenza if you'd like. My state also required an inspection of my farm and hatching facilities, but not all states require this. Currently all the major hatcheries in the US participate in the program. Many breeders have also joined the NPIP program. Again, it is a volunteer program and just because a flock is in the program and regularly tested does not mean they are clean of every disease. Conversely, just because a flock isn't in the program does not mean that it's not clean of diseases.

I've found that being able to use the NPIP logo has loaned credibility to my farm operation but has not been useful outside of that. Certain states require NPIP paperwork to accompany chicks or hatching eggs being shipped into or out of their state. Complete details can be found at the NPIP website: www.poultryimprovement.org

Growing your business

With all these different methods of promoting your chick business you're going to need a way to keep track of everything. You'll need to take notes when you talk to people about purchasing or ordering chicks. These notes will be invaluable when you find yourself with more chicks than you thought would hatch and can't remember who it was that said they were interested. It doesn't need to be anything fancy, just a notepad will do. As long as all your notes are in one place, so you can check them when needed.

You'll need a calendar to keep track of different swaps or auctions. A calendar is also necessary when planning out your hatches. As soon as I set the eggs I write down what is hatching and when, in both my notebook and my calendar. When people contact me about buying chicks I can easily tell them when they can expect their order to be ready. It also helps to write down their name, contact info and how many chicks they want on that date. This helps me to keep a running total of what's sold and what is still available. I also have a calendar on my phone. I use this to make notes of any unsold birds and their expected hatch dates, so I have the information with me when someone asks about chicks.

I use hatching software to keep track of all my hatches. I've been using the free phone app by Brinsea, although I do have hatching software on my computer also. There are several different companies that make hatching software, or you can simply use a whiteboard calendar and write it out by hand. No matter what method you use, it's important that you keep track of exactly what is hatching and when.

To keep track of hatches, I assign each hatch a number when I set the eggs. I write the number on the eggs with pencil, and label the trays or the incubator. Use whatever method works for you as long as there is no question as to which eggs go with which hatch. In my notebook I record the day I set the eggs and what day the eggs will move into the hatcher or go into lockdown. I set an alert in the software or an alarm on my phone to let me know when it's time to move the eggs to the hatching area. It also helps if you set eggs on the same day every week. If you hatch week after week or even every two weeks, then you'll get into the habit of setting eggs or putting eggs in lockdown on the same day every week.

Name recognition

You should choose a name for your chick hatching business and use it in all your ads, advertising materials, and social media profiles. You can make something up or use your own name, whichever you prefer. Do some research before choosing your name. Look around locally and online and see if your name is being used already. If the name is being used by another farm (even if it's not in your area) choose differently to avoid confusing customers. If you think you might want to have a website, make sure the domain name is available first. GoDaddy has a search tool you can use to check if a URL is available.

Once you've chosen a name, you'll use this name on your Facebook, Instagram, Twitter, etc. accounts. Make sure you use the same name for everything. You want customers to recognize that name and know right away who you are. You should also set up an email address for all your farm messages. It takes a little bit of time to set it all up in the beginning but it's worth it when you start getting direct messages from people wanting to order chicks from you.

To minimize your expenses, you're going to want the chicks sold the day after they hatch. If you get stuck raising chicks for weeks then you're going to put feed, electric and time into them. Not only is that costing you money, but your time is valuable also. Preferably you will have people waiting on each hatch. In the beginning you'll have to find your buyers but as time goes by and you become well known, they'll begin to find you. Here are some places I've promoted/sold chicks that have worked for me:

- Facebook
- Instagram
- Twitter
- Craigslist
- Blog

Facebook

I recommend making a 'like page' so people that buy from you can follow the page on Facebook. While it's tempting to just use your personal Facebook profile, if you get reported, facebook can close your profile, so it's best to make a page. Join local groups. There are a lot of local poultry swap groups on Facebook, find some and join them. These groups usually have information on when and where different poultry swaps and chicken based events are being held. If you can't find a local group, you could start your own group. I started a local Farm & Garden group that has a decent number of members and everyone posts chicks and other farm items we have for sale. These groups are also a great place to get ideas about which breeds people are looking for and which ones everyone seems to have. Because Facebook just changed their animal policy, you might have to do most of your transactions through direct messages.

Instagram

IG is easy to use because you simply upload a photo of whatever chicks you currently have. Like with Facebook, you will get followers from all over the world so make sure you have your location (city and state only) in your profile. When uploading a photo to Instagram use a clear photo of the chicks you currently have for sale. Add the location to the photo at the top. Photos with the location added get 80% more views. The location helps locals to find you and that is exactly who your main customer is. Choose your city, township or county for the location. Do not put in your exact address. Once a chick has sold, do not remove the photo simply edit the caption to say 'sold, message me for details on next hatch' or something like that. You want the picture to stay up so customers can see what types of chicks you have. Add some relevant hashtags to your posts to help it show up in searches. I hashtag the breed and my location plus a few general chicken or homesteading terms. I've had a lot of locals find me on Instagram and buy chicks. Instagram is my second top referrer for chick sales.

Twitter

Twitter is a little harder to use for chick sales because it moves very fast! I had the best results when I added a photo to my tweets. The hashtag was born on twitter and it will still help people to find you. Use a hashtag for your location and descriptive words. The important thing to remember about social media is the number of followers matters a whole lot less than the quality of followers. If you only have 6 followers but they buy from you whenever they see your posts, that's much better then hundreds of followers that never buy from you.

Craigslist & More

Agricultural animal sales are allowed on Craigslist in the **Farm & Garden** section only. I place ads on the closest Craigslist board to my location, but I occasionally post in other areas within a few hours drive. You'll be surprised how far people are willing to drive when they really want a certain breed of chicks! Always use pictures in your listings. Listings with pictures get a much higher rate of views than ones without pictures.

Ads should also be placed on other local flea market or

agricultural sites. Both local and national boards can be utilized to find buyers. I post on every free site I can find even if a site does not seem to get a great deal of traffic. You never know who's going to see the ad and give you a call. Check your ads every few months and repost if they've fallen too far down the list or have become inactive. National chicken sites like Backyard Chickens also have sections you can list your chicks or eggs in. Specify that you do not ship if you choose to not ship chicks or eggs.

Blog

A blog does not have to be complex to be effective. You can use a free blog platform, there's no need to invest in it at this point. As long as you can post pictures and text about which birds you currently have or are expecting, then that is all you need. There are multiple free platforms like Google's Blogger, Wordpress.com, Typepad, Weebly, Squarespace and Webs.com that will work just fine for a farm blog.

Finding your buyers in person

- ☐ Putting signs up
- ☐ Handing out business cards
- ☐ Word of mouth
- ☐ Poultry swaps
- ☐ Poultry auctions
- ☐ Feed Stores

Post signs at feed stores, pet stores and veterinarian offices

Make a sign on your computer and print it out. You can get them copied cheaply at a copy place. Keep some in your car so you always have them with you. It's best to ask permission before you put up signs unless it's a designated area like a community bulletin board. The signs should include what you'll have available and how to contact you. Make sure the type is large enough to be read several feet away, you want it to catch a potential customer's eye. Add a picture if you can. Some people like to make little tear tabs with their phone number printed on the bottom. Keep scotch tape and push pins with the signs in your car so you always have what you need to put them up.

Business cards

I also carry a box of business cards in my truck, so I always have some to put up whenever I see a community bulletin board. They have these types of boards at most feed stores, coffee shops, small diners and grocery stores. Anywhere you see a bulletin board, stick some cards up. You never know who may come along and pick up a card or pass it on to someone else. Ask if you can leave a stack of cards on the counter at local feed stores.

Business cards can be ordered online cheaply. Many sites sell 1,000 for under $10. Have the following information on it: your farm name, phone number and email address, what types of animals you offer, and the URL to any online profiles you have pictures on. Instagram, Facebook etc. People are very visual, and many like to browse before they commit to buy so adding your profiles gives them a chance to do that.

Word of mouth

If you give your customers a good buying experience, they will tell other people about you and you'll gain new customers. Keep in mind if you give them a bad experience they will still tell people about you! Treat each customer as if you want to see them again and you probably will! Return customers truly are the best customers.

Poultry swaps

'Buy, sell and trade' should actually be the name of these

events. You don't have to swap chickens. You can attend a poultry swap just to buy a few hens or sell some chicks. Some people do trade, but it's not just chickens. Most swaps also have ducks, guineas, peafowl, quail, geese and chukars. Many swaps also allow other farm animals like goats, lambs, pigs, and rabbits. Some sellers will also bring things they make like nest boxes, coops, killing cones, or feeders. You can find a whole lot of interesting stuff at a chicken swap.

Some swaps provide tents and roped off areas, others just let people set up wherever they decide to park their vehicles. Think of it like a flea market for farm critters. Most sellers don't bring tables, but some do. Some set up on their tailgates, in their trunk spaces or inside their hatchback cars. I like to bring my pickup truck and put a row of cages across the tailgate and another row on the ground in front of the tailgate (I use a tarp under my cages to keep them off the ground, but not everybody does).

Some people like to haggle and make deals, others don't. Some just brought a few extra chickens to get rid of, some are hobbyists, some are business owners. You can find show quality stock or pet quality. You get a little of everything and that's always a good thing.

It's a good place to get rid of extras if they're not purebred, especially if you price them right. Your missing hen suddenly appeared with 15 chicks? Have a roo go rogue and break into a breeding pen and now your hatching cross-breed chicks? Put a $2 each sign on them and they'll be sold out in no time!

Poultry Auction

You can make good money on poultry auctions, but they can be hit or miss. You never know what you're going to get for anything you take there. Selling chickens at auction is different every time depending who's there to buy, what they're looking for and what else is there to sell. The great part about poultry auctions though, is that many of them run year-round. So those are an excellent option for slower months and you won't have much competition then either.

The most important thing I learned about poultry auctions is to separate your chicks into small groups. You'll usually get a higher price for 3 sets of 5 chicks than you will for 1 set of 15 chicks. Many people are individual buyers not farms. They're not always permitted to have unlimited amounts of chickens, or they just don't have the space. They will pay more for a small lot because they don't want to get stuck with extras. When packing chicks for auction, put each set in their own box with bedding. On the outside of the box, use a marker to write how many chicks are in the box. Most likely the chicks will stay in the box until auction time, so put at least a few chicks in each box for warmth. The auctions I've been to do not have a heated or air conditioned holding area. Make sure to poke plenty of ventilation holes in summer, and maybe throw a hand warmer in with them in winter.

Chickens over a few months old sell better individually or in pairs. Many auctions have temporary cage blocks that they move full grown birds into for better viewing. Make sure your chickens are in good health before taking them to auction. Not only is that the right thing to do because of their proximity to so many other chickens, but healthy looking birds can fetch a higher price.

Feed store accounts

After I joined the NPIP I approached local feed stores about selling my chicks. Several of them agreed to give my cards out to people inquiring about chicks and I got many sales from them. One feed store preferred to take orders then call me to fill them. Since they often ordered 50 chicks or keets at a time I would give them a volume discount. Obviously, there's more money to be made by selling to the public directly, but it's very convenient to get rid of a whole hatch in one sale.

Hold policies

I learned the hard way that I needed to decide on a hold policy and stick to it. The idea behind selling the chicks right away is that I don't have to spend money for feed, electric for the heat lamp and time on caring for chicks. I do have a brooder set up and ready, but I want all the chicks sold within a few days of hatch. I don't want to hold them indefinitely until the buyer makes time to get them. I'd rather sell them and move the buyer down the list to the next hatch.

Unfortunately, I've had people purposely put me off for weeks! Of the ones that did it on purpose, most just didn't feel a sense of urgency since they knew the chicks were waiting for them. Meeting to pick them up fell to the bottom of their 'to do' list. I do understand, but it's a lot more work and expense for me. A few did it on purpose because they wanted older chicks. I don't sell older chicks because they usually sell as soon as they hatch, and I tell people this when they ask. Having me hold the chicks "just one more week" several times was a way for them to get around that. It didn't happen that much, but it was enough for me to create a hold policy.

There are times when something really does come up for a customer and I am still slightly flexible. I now offer 2 variations of the hold policy.

1) No holds. If chicks are not picked up after 1 week they

will be sold and you will be moved to the next hatch. Hatches are usually every week, so they never have to wait long. I do allow people to pick their hatch dates when they order if they have a vacation or something to work around. They can contact me and switch to a later hatch date if something comes up.

2) Holds with cost increase. In this instance I will hold your chicks for up to 3 weeks at a cost of $1 a week per chick. This works well for custom hatches.

Personal Safety

If you advertise online and somebody contacts you for chicks you should meet them with the chicks in a public place. If you're selling 50 chicks a week you will be meeting with a lot of people and having them all come to your house is not such a good idea. Not only is that unsafe for you, but if that many people are visiting your farm, the biosecurity of your birds can be compromised.

No matter what, do not put your address online. If people find your address online, they will show up unannounced. You wouldn't want people to be wandering your property when you're not there, so make sure you only use a phone number and email address for your contact information. I've learned this the hard way and there are many times I went outside to see why the dogs were barking and someone I've never seen before was standing in my driveway. I often wonder how many times this happened when I wasn't home. It's not a good risk to take, so I no longer have my address listed online.

If somebody makes you feel uncomfortable about meeting them it's ok to say no or take another person with you. Don't ever feel pressured to sell to someone who makes you feel uncomfortable.

Biosecurity

Biosecurity is a pattern of behaviors designed to prevent the spread of disease onto your farm. To protect your chickens, you'll need to limit visitors from other farms to prevent them from bringing diseases to your chickens. This goes hand in hand with personal safety as we discussed in the last chapter. If a customer has an infected flock at home and drives off their property they carry the disease with them. Bacteria can be on their shoes, tires and possibly their hands. When they drive onto your property, they can be spreading the disease. By keeping people off your farm, you keep both yourself and your animals safe.

You could also be picking up that disease and taking it home with you in places like farm shows, poultry swaps, and auctions! With the recent outbreaks of Avian Influenza you just can't be too careful! Here are the steps I take whenever I attend a poultry swap or show. These are steps that I believe we should all follow to keep our flocks safe.

1) Hand sanitizer:

Bring the kind with a pump top and use it between people or birds. Shake someone's hand? Sanitize after. Pick up a bird to look at? Sanitize again. Don't forget to use it before entering your vehicle after leaving the poultry swap. You can buy big bottles of sanitizer at dollar stores.

The active ingredient is alcohol, which is cheap anyway, so brand name doesn't usually matter.

2) Shoes and tires:

I always wash my vehicle and shoes on the drive home. Everybody drives their vehicles on their own property, right? Tires pick up dirt, mud, poop....whatever they drive through. Shoes accumulate germs and yuck also. It's safe to say that if a flock has a disease in it there will be germs on their property. If somebody drives through something nasty on their property, then I drive after them at the swap or auction parking lot, it is possible to pick up whatever they may have. It's not likely, but it's possible. Also, I have seen birds running around at swaps when people take them out to look at them and they get loose. If I walk through some bird poo then whatever that bird has is coming home with me. That's another reason to visit the car wash. I either wear boots I can scrub off, or flip flops I can take off as I get back in the truck. I stick the flip flops in a plastic bag and scrub with bleach when I get home. (Wash them in the sink, not the hose!)

3) Tarps:

Always, ALWAYS put a tarp down before you put a cage on the ground at a swap. Do you have any idea what was in the last cage that was put in that spot? Or the one before that? Of course you don't. Better safe than sorry.

You can buy the small 5'x7' tarps for under $3 at the home improvement store or even at the dollar store. Generally, if I use these I just throw them away after. You can buy a larger tarp at any big box store. These I wash at the car wash before I get home, then wash again with Oxine AH or bleach solution at home. Always roll your tarp inwards when you clean up. Take your birdy poo with you. Also, keep the tarp folded under the cages as much as possible. Don't leave enough hanging out that someone can step on it or even trip over the edges.

4) Tubs:

Rubbermaid tubs that is. I suppose metal tubs would work too. Whichever you choose, if you can't put a tarp down make sure there is a solid bottom between the birds and the ground. These also can be washed at the carwash on the way home. They contain poo well, but should only be used for chicks or ducklings that cannot fly yet since you'll need to leave the lid off for air circulation.

5) Empty cages/full boxes & signs:

I come to the poultry swap with empty cages in the back of my truck. The birds are all in boxes in the back seat. I take out some of each breed to put in the cages and replenish as needed. If someone asks I tell them what else I have. I also have a small dry erase board and I write what breeds I have and the prices on it. The birds that never leave the boxes in the truck cab are never exposed to anything and can be returned to their home brooders if they don't sell. The ones that make it into the cages either need to be quarantined when they get back home ... or better yet, sell them before I leave! Sometimes I make deals at the end of the day to save myself the issue of quarantine. Unsold birds get put back in boxes *together* for the ride home. They are never mixed with the ones that didn't make it to the cages. The liquor stores will give you all the boxes you need if you call ahead and ask when you can pick up.

6) Change your clothes:

When I get home that is. At this point I've driven through the car wash, hosed off my cages, and disposed of my tarps (or pre-washed the big ones). If I wore boots, I take them off in the driveway. I go into the house and change and throw those clothes in the washer before touching anything.

7) Putting it all away clean:

After I'm all changed, I put away the birds that never left the truck cab and set up the quarantine area. Then I put on rubber gloves and take the boxes of birds that had made it to the cages and put them in quarantine. I burn the rubber gloves and the boxes those birds used. I take everything out of the back of the truck and put it in the driveway. Spray down the cages and big tarps with Oxine or bleach solution, let sit for about 15 minutes then hose off. Don't forget to do the flip side. If I wore boots (and pre-washed them at the car wash) they also get the cleaning solution and wash. If I took off my shoes when I entered the truck they get washed in the laundry tub with bleach.

While this is a bit of extra work, I operate with the 'better safe than sorry' motto. To me these steps make perfect sense and it only takes a few extra minutes.

Alternative sales methods

If you live in the southern half of the country, you can probably sell chicks almost year-round. If your hatching more then you are selling though, you may want to slow down on hatching and supplement your chick income with some of these other ideas.

Hatching eggs

You can sell hatching eggs locally or you can sell them online and ship the eggs throughout the country. Unfortunately, you cannot ship hatching eggs out of the country. For me the demand for chicks is lower locally in the winter but I can still get $3 to $4 per egg in online egg auctions. I have used both chicken sites and EBay to sell hatching eggs. The difference here is that you're selling all the eggs, not just the ones that hatch. That is why I set my per egg price lower.

There are 2 types of online egg sales. Set price and auctions. With a set price you are guaranteed a certain amount when your eggs sell. With an auction, you can choose a minimum start price and you may end up getting much more money for your eggs then you thought! I prefer auctions. Eggs are a perishable item. You can't hold onto them for a few months until you find the right buyer. They need to get sold right away or they start losing viability. With an auction you are at least guaranteed your minimum price.

To pack hatching eggs you'll want to first wrap them in strips of bubble wrap. I use the bubble wrap with the small bubbles for this. Secure with tape on the sides, top and bottom. Place in an extra-large egg carton with the top cut off. Place the top on and secure it to the bottom with tape. I use clear packing tape. Wrap the carton with a few sheets of bubble wrap. I like to use the wrap with the big bubbles for this. Secure with tape. Get a flat rate box from USPS and put a layer of Styrofoam peanuts or other filler in the bottom. Place the egg carton in the box diagonally, on top of the packing peanuts. Fill in the corners with more packing peanuts or wadded up bubble wrap. Top with bubble wrap and tape securely shut. Make sure the box is full enough that the egg carton does not get jostled around.

I write **fragile** and **this side up** on the box, but I honestly find that it makes no difference. Some people like to write **"do not x-ray, live embryos"**. There is no actual evidence as to whether this keeps the box from being X-rayed or not, so I see it as a personal preference. If you have NPIP paperwork, you'll attach this to the outside of the box. Ship priority mail and make sure you request a signature.

Eating eggs

Selling fresh eggs for eating will bring the lowest price, but it still a viable option to bring in some money with your eggs. There are some rules and regulations that must be followed though.

Laws first:

Look up your state laws. You can find the local rules on your state department of agriculture website. The rules on backyard egg sales seem to change fairly often so you should check them at least yearly for any changes. You could do a web search for 'your state' egg sales. These rules often include how to package eggs, temperatures for storage, how quickly you must sell them and what information you must include.

Collecting your eggs:

It's important that you collect the eggs from the coop every single day. This is even more important in the summer when fertile eggs can start to develop if left outside in high temperatures for too long. "Too long" in this case, is more than 24 hours. Make sure they're brought in out of the heat daily.

Packaging:

I've seen some really adorable packaging setups for farm fresh eggs. I've also seen eggs be offered in just a plain blank egg carton. In some states you must use new cartons and in others you can reuse clean egg cartons, this information should be in with the other rules for your state. Whatever you decide to do, consistency is important. It's also important to have either a label or business card attached to them so that people know how to get in touch with you to order more eggs. If you live in a state where reusing cartons is allowed, make sure you mark off any manufacturer's info like the date stamp on the end and the company name.

You could order fancy eggs stamps and egg container liners and things like that. I don't think they're necessary. They're also an added expense. However, expenses are deductible when you do your taxes at the end of the year so that would be completely up to you if you think it's worth it. I will say the memorable packaging can help you get the sale at places like farmers markets where customers are browsing.

Pricing:

Figuring out how to price your hens' eggs can be tricky. You can't use the grocery stores as a guideline at all. You won't be able to compete with their low pricing, and they can't compete with your quality. You could check the prices on organic free range eggs in your store and use that as a guideline, if your store carries those! Your best bet is to try to figure out what price people are already paying for the same product in your area. Visiting a farmer's market or small farm store should give you an idea of what to charge.

Your motive for selling eggs can also help determine what to charge for them. If you just don't want them to go to waste or want to put a dent in the feed bill, then a low price might be good for your situation, especially if you want to move them fast! If you're looking to start making money off your eggs, then you'll want to charge more. Sometimes charging more can mean heading into the city where fresh eggs are more of a rarity.

Decide where to sell:

This brings us back to those state regulations. You may be allowed to sell from your home only or not at all. Many states allow for farmers market sales. Find out if you're allowed to sell from your home and if so a "fresh eggs" sign hung at the end of your driveway might be all you need. If you're getting enough fresh eggs to stock a whole stand then a farmer's market may be right for you. You could also consider cutting out the footwork and going to a gourmet restaurant and sell eggs directly to them.

Once customers get a taste for your eggs they will be coming back again and again for more. Make sure you let them know if you're not going to be able to provide eggs for them in low production times so it doesn't come as a surprise. My customers all know that I don't have eating eggs during hatching season.

Be careful with your descriptions:

Terms like free range eggs or cage free hens are regulated terms. In order to use these terms you have to get approval from the FSIS (Food Safety and Inspection Service). It's a complex process so I would suggest using non-regulated terms like 'naturally raised' or 'from happy backyard chickens'. If you want to get into all the details though, it's on the FDAs website. I know this seems like a lot, but making sure you follow the rules in the beginning can save a lot of headaches for you in the long run!

Feathers

You can sell your chickens feathers. I pick dropped feathers up all the time and by using this method to gather them I can label them as cruelty free, which many people like to see. I also clip the hackle, tail and saddle feathers of any chicken that happens to pass on while living here. I wash them gently and sell them online for craft projects, hair clips and fly fishing. Guinea feathers are great for this too since people adore the spots. EBay and Etsy both allow feather sales. You can also sell them privately to crafters through Craigslist or Facebook groups and even craft shows.

Chicken Manure

Organic gardeners will pay for chicken poop. They prefer aged manure with or without coop bedding mixed in, depending on the buyer. I have found buyers through Craigslist and on Facebook in local gardening groups. I store it in feed bags and charge about $20 a bag. Depending on how much free range time my chickens get, I fill up about a bag a week if not more. It's not a large amount of money but it does add up.

Expenses

Once you have your breeding groups going your only expenses should be feed, coop litter and electric. On my blog www.MuranoChickenFarm.com I often write about saving money on feed. If your feed expenses seem higher than they should be, visit my blog and read some of the dozen posts on cutting feed costs to see how you can lower the feed bill. Other than feed, your biggest 'expense' is going to be your time.

On average I spend about an hour a day doing chicken chores. This includes everything from feeding and watering to spot cleaning coops. One weekend a month I spend about 3 hours doing more in-depth chores like deep cleaning, scrubbing bowls, and repairing fences and such. As I mentioned in the beginning of the book, this is geared towards people that already had chickens before deciding to make money with them. These are all standard chicken keeping chores. I don't really consider this a time expense since it's all things I must do to own chickens anyway.

The time I spend focused on selling chicks is time I could be doing other things though, so this is a business 'time expense'. Some people don't mind the time expense at all and will happily work on chick sales all day long. I did that for quite a few years so if you want to spend hours and hours on advertising and meeting people by all means, go for it! If, however you want to cut your time down to a minimum this next section is for you. This is how I learned to handle the business when I got stuck in a time crunch.

I spend about an hour a week answering emails, posting to groups and online bulletin boards and making phone calls. I rotate between where I post and keep lists of everyone that is interested in buying chicks. If you're selling chicks every week you'll find that people will often call about an ad from months ago, so you really don't need to post in every place, every week. Instead of posting a new ad in an online group you can often bump an ad to pop it back up to the top of the forum by posting a new comment on it. Don't post 'bump' though, it's spammy. Just think of something new to say, add a picture of the new hatch or comment that more are hatching this week. Also, take new pictures for your ads every few weeks. Just a few seconds snapping a pic with your cell phone makes it a whole new ad, and helps to attract new interest.

Auctions and swaps command a block of time of course, but I only do maybe 2 a month. If I have enough direct sales I don't bother with these. With these events you must determine if it's worth the time and money before you go. If you only have 5 extra chicks, it'll cost you very little in feed to hang on to them a few more days. It would cost you time and gas to drive to the auction or swap. In that instance it will probably be cheaper to hang onto them till you find a buyer. However, if you have 20 extra chicks then it would certainly be worthwhile to take them to a swap or auction. The auctions I go to have drop off hours and they send out checks afterwards, so those take very little time. Location is important also. If you're driving in that direction anyway then there isn't much of a time expense. You need to balance it all out or you'll find yourself constantly running around which takes all your time and eats into your profits with fuel costs. Though you'll have to spend some time at swaps, they can be a good place to make contacts. If it feels like you're running low on customers, take some chicks to a swap and do some networking. Don't forget to hand out cards to anyone you talk to.

When meeting people to sell chicks, I try to meet them all in the same block of time and at the same place. This keeps my time expense down to a minimum. Since I don't live in a populated area it works out well to just meet everyone in town on the day I'm going into town anyway. If you live close by you may be ok with meeting people whenever they want. Whatever works for you obviously.

When packing up to meet customers, I separate orders of chicks into boxes. I label the box with what's inside, the agreed-on price and the buyer's name & phone number. It's important to put all the info directly on the box so you don't get confused by trying to remember details of several transactions as they're happening. I get a pile of free boxes at the liquor store or grocery store every few weeks. They're usually happy to have someone take boxes off their hands, but you may need to go on their specific stocking day. Ask around, I'm sure you'll find someone who needs to get rid of boxes. Keep a stack of boxes and some filler like wood shavings or shredded newspaper on hand. Some people like to put a hand warmer in the box with the chicks. Unless it's a cold day or they're going to be in the box a long time, I don't worry about it. Being organized will make it very easy to meet with multiple customers and be done quickly.

I can usually meet with all my customers within 2 hours a week. I spend about an hour a week setting eggs, candling them and cleaning out the incubator or hatcher between hatches. I would say I average between 4-6 hours a week handling chick sales in one way or another.

Taxes

I'm sure that it's no surprise that you are expected to pay taxes on your income. I recommend you hire an accountant in your area who has dealt with farms extensively. Our first year filing business taxes, we went to a well-known farm accountant who advised us on what we could and could not do. In the first appointment he provided us a wealth of information based on his experiences. An accountant familiar with agricultural businesses is worth a lot more then you'll pay him!

At the very least have a professional explain them to you. Many expenses like feed and certain equipment are deductible. Some things that you think should be deductible may not be. I save every receipt and organize them by month and type then let my account approve what is allowed. I have done my own taxes a few times after learning from the accountant and once you have a good grasp of what is allowed and what's not allowed, it becomes much easier.

Please don't make the mistake of thinking because it is a cash only business that you will not get caught. If you are advertising online and using tax exempt status, there is enough of a paper trail that leads to you.

In closing

Chances are you already have chickens and an incubator and would like to get started right away. If you have a rooster in your flock, then you can hatch chicks. While they might not be purebred you can still sell them, though you won't be able to charge as much for them. If you're new to incubation this could be great practice while you get your flock in order.

Since writing the original blog post that inspired this book I have received many messages, comments and even a few calls on the topic. Many people were excited to share their successes with me since starting to hatch and sell chicks. I am so excited for every one of them! It's particularly heartwarming to read about the ones who have made enough money to pay the feed bills that month. That's really all I ever intended to do, and it thrills me to no end to be able to help other do that too!

The only mistake I'm seeing is jumping in too quickly. Deciding to hatch chicks today and setting dozens of eggs every week without doing breed research and finding the customers first. Then when the chicks start hatching it becomes hard to find the buyers to support it. Don't be afraid to take it slow. I started with 3 guineas the first year. I added 8 more that fall, then added another 34 the next fall for a total of 45 guineas in my flock. 45 still wasn't enough at that point but had I tried to start out with that many the first year, my experience would not have gone well!

Don't be afraid to raise your prices if you can. If you have great quality purebred chicks, you can hatch half as many and still make the same money by charging more. If your chicks are worth it, people will pay it. It's definitely worth your time and effort to work on your breed and constantly improve your quality.

Enjoy your new chick hatching adventure. I certainly have enjoyed the last 8 years and at no point did it feel like work. That is kind of my life's goal...to make money without feeling like I'm working. This has been more of an adventure than a job.

Good luck to you! ~Lisa

Glossary of incubation terms

Air cell: The pocket of air inside the egg at the large end. The air cell gets larger as incubation progresses.

Albumen: The egg white.

Blastoderm: This is the nucleus of the egg when it is fertilized. Seen on the yolk.

Blastodisc: This is the nucleus of the egg when it is

unfertilized. Seen on the yolk.

Blood Ring: A line or ring of blood inside an egg that has started to develop into a chick but quit at an early stage.

Bloom: The protective coating on freshly laid eggs that helps seal the pores of the egg shell. This prevents bacteria from entering the egg. Also called the cuticle.

Broody: A hen that is sitting on a clutch of eggs in order to hatch them into chicks.

Candle: Looking inside an egg to see the contents by using a bright light source.

Candler: The light used to see inside the egg.

Candling: The act of looking inside the egg with a bright light source.

Clutch: The group of eggs a hen decides to collect before becoming broody and hatching them.

Embryo: The developing chick while in the egg.

Forced Air: Having a fan inside an incubator forcing the air to circulate.

Germinal Disc: The fertilization site in the egg, on the yolk. Also called blastoderm or blastodisc.

Hatch: The process of the chick getting itself out of the egg.

Hatch Rate: Percentage of eggs that hatched into chicks. If 9 out of 10 hatch, your hatch rate is 90%

Humidity: Amount of water vapor in the air inside the incubator.

Hygrometer: Device used to measure humidity.

Incubation: Subjecting the eggs to ideal hatching conditions for the proper amount of time while controlling heat and humidity in order to hatch chicks.

Incubation Period: Amount of time each egg takes to develop completely. Example, chickens have a 21 day incubation period while ducks have a 28 day incubation period.

Incubator: Object used to incubate eggs which holds in heat and humidity.

Infertile Egg: Egg that has not been fertilized.

Lockdown: The last 3 days of incubation when humidity is raised to the proper level and the incubator is not to be opened to prevent the loss of humidity.

Membrane: A thin, skin like coating surrounding the albumen. There are actually 2 membranes, but you'll only be dealing with the inner shell membrane ... around the egg white. The outer shell membrane sticks to the inside of the shell.

Pip: The first little break a chick makes through the membrane and shell. The first step in hatching.

Quitter: An egg that has quit developing at some point during the incubation period.

Set: The act of putting the eggs in the incubator to start the incubation process.

Shrink Wrapped: When the membrane of a hatching chick becomes too dry and it shrinks around the chick. Often it inhibits movement to the point that the chick cannot move to continue hatching causing death.

Still Air: The air inside an incubator without any artificial air circulation.

Temperature: The degree of heat present inside the incubator.

Thermometer: Object that measures the degree of heat inside the incubator.

Turn or turning Eggs: Rotating eggs several times a day to keep the chick forming uniformly

Turner: Rack or device inside incubator on a timer that turns eggs for you.

Zip: After the pip, the process of turning inside the egg while breaking through the shell repeatedly in order to be able to remove the top of the egg and hatch out of it.

Made in the
USA
Monee, IL